JOHN DRYDEN.

MAYNARD'S ENGLISH CLASSIC SERIES.—No. 39.

ALEXANDER'S FEAST,

MACFLECKNOE,

AND

ST. CECILIA'S DAY.

BY

JOHN DRYDEN.

WITH PHILOLOGICAL AND EXPLANATORY NOTES

BY

J. W. HALES, M.A.

LATE FELLOW AND ASSISTANT TUTOR OF CHRIST'S COLLEGE, CAMBRIDGE;
BARRISTER-AT-LAW OF LINCOLN'S INN;
LECTURER IN ENGLISH LITERATURE AND CLASSICAL COMPOSITION AT KING'S
COLLEGE SCHOOL, LONDON; CO-EDITOR OF BISHOP PERCY'S
MS. FOLIO; ETC.

NEW YORK

CHARLES E. MERRILL CO.

BIOGRAPHY.

1. JOHN DRYDEN was born on the 5th of August, 1631, probably in the house of his maternal grandfather, at Aldwincle,
All Saints, near Oundle, in Northamptonshire, Eng. His father
was the proprietor of a small estate at Blakesley. In course of
time he was sent to Westminster School, then under the super-
intendence of Dr. Busby, and subsequently to Trinity College,
Cambridge. Leaving the University in 1657, without, it would
seem, having specially distinguished himself there, he went up
to London, and devoted himself to politics and to literature.
Amongst his family connections were certain important members
of the Puritan party. The death of Cromwell soon provided him
with a poetical subject. His writing an elegy on that occasion did
not prevent him, any more than Waller, and other poets of the
day, from welcoming back with a poem Charles the Second.
With the Restoration a new field was thrown open to the wits
of the time in the shape of the stage, which for some eighteen
years had been altogether, or partially shut up. Dryden turned
play-writer. He wrote comedies, tragedies, tragi-comedies : the
comedies in prose; the tragedies, the earliest in blank verse,
then some in rhyme, on the model of the French tragic drama ;
the latest in blank verse. His subjects he drew mostly from the
old romances, and from history. He reproduced three of
Shakespeare's plays, *Troilus and Cressida*, *Antony and Cleopatra*
(which he called *All for Love*), and *The Tempest*. In 1671 his
plays were heartily, and not undeservedly, ridiculed in the *Rehearsal*, written by the Duke of Buckingham, assisted, it is said,
by "Hudibras" Butler, and others. All this time he was winning more lasting fame by the various critical essays with which
his plays, when published, were frequently prefaced. In 1663
he married the Lady Elizabeth Howard, a daughter of the Earl
of Berkshire, who by no means proved a congenial consort.

2. It was not till Dryden was some fifty years old that he
fully discovered where his strength lay. Before 1681 he had
written other poetical pieces, as his *Annus Mirabilis* (published
in 1667, the same year with *Paradise Lost*), besides his plays, and
everything he had written had been marked by a certain power
and might ; but in that year his *Absalom and Achitophel* displayed

3

his characteristic talents in their fullest and completest vigor
The nation was at that time in a state of profound excitement;
the struggle between Absolutism and Constitutionalism was
rapidly nearing its final crisis; the contest between the Court
party and the Exclusionists, an important passage in that other
all-comprehensive struggle, had just reached its utmost fury.
Dryden stood forth as the champion of the Court party; in his
Absalom and Achitophel he dealt the Exclusionists the severest
blows his genius could inflict, and they were terribly effective.
That poem was speedily followed by another, *The Medal*, aimed
at the same Achitophel; and this by another, *Mac Flecknoe*,
aimed at Shadwell, the chief poet of the Whig side. At this
same memorable period of his life he wrote also *Religio Laici*, to
vindicate Revelation against Atheism, and Protestantism against
Tradition. How well the Stuarts rewarded his great services
appears from the fact that it was only with much appealing and
difficulty he could procure the payment of the salary due to
him as Poet Laureate. Not long after the succession of James
II. he became a Roman Catholic; with his usual fervor and brill-
iancy he in 1686 wrote his *Hind and Panther* (published the following year), in which he defended that tradition of which in
the *Religio Laici* he had made so light. When the boy was born
who was afterwards known as "the Pretender," Dryden celebrated the event in his *Britannia Rediviva;* but that birth was in
fact the signal for the combined action of a justly indignant
nation, and the irreparable fall of the Stuart dynasty.

3. Dryden fell with his patrons. Whatever may be thought
of the consistency of his previous life, he certainly refused
overtures now made to him by the triumphant Protestant party.
His political life ended; his literary activity was as intense as
ever. He now set himself to the translation of certain classical
poets. His version of Persius and Juvenal was published in
1693; that of the *Æneid* in 1697, in which same year he wrote
also his now best-known poem, his *Alexander's Feast*. His
modernizations of Chaucer and other pieces—his *Fables*—appeared in 1700. Thus his vigor remained to the end, for in 1700
he died.

Of his twenty-eight plays scarcely any one is now at all known,
and perhaps not much more deserves to be known. The comedies
abound in wit, those written in the heroic metre in fine versifi-
cation; but Dryden was wanting in dramatic power, he was
wanting in humor, in tenderness, in delicacy. He could de-

scribe in a masterly manner, but this is not the dramatist's great function; he had not the art of making his characters develop themselves—describe themselves by their actions so to speak. He could lay bare all the motives that actuated them, but he could not show them in a state of action obedient to those motives; in short, his power was rather of the analytical kind.

His descriptive power was of the highest. Our literature has in it no more vigorous portrait-gallery than that he has bequeathed it. He succeeds better in his portraits of enemies than of friends; perhaps, because, as it happened, the Whig leaders excited in him more disgust than the Tories admiration. The general type of character which that age presented was in an eminent degree calculated not to stir enthusiasm. Dryden fell upon evil times. What he for the most part saw was flagrant corruption in Church and in State, and in society. He lived the best years of his life in the most infamous period of English history; he was getting old when a better time began. The poet reflects his age; there was but little noble for Dryden to reflect. Naturally, he turned satirist.

His power of expression is beyond praise. There is always a singular *fitness* in his language; he uses always the right word.

He is one of our greatest masters of metre: metre was, in fact, no restraint to him, but rather it seems to have given him freedom. It has been observed that he argues better in verse than in prose: verse was the natural costume of his thoughts. As a prose-writer he is excellent; but verse-writing was his proper province.

Note.—In this number of the English Classics it has been thought desirable to copy the orthography of the author, that the student may see the changes made since his time.

ALEXANDER'S FEAST.

OR, THE POWER OF MUSIC.

Introductory Note.—This song was written in 1697, in a single night, according to St. John, afterwards Lord Bolingbroke. He states that Dryden said to him when he called upon him one morning: " I have been up all night: my musical friends made me promise to write them an Ode for their Feast of St. Cecilia, and I was so struck with the subject which occurred to me that I could not leave it till I had completed it; here it is, finished at one sitting."

I.

'Twas at the royal feast for Persia won
  By Philip's warlike son,
    Aloft in awful state
    The godlike hero sate
    On his imperial throne;   5
His valiant peers were plac'd around,
Their brows with roses and with myrtles bound;
(So shou'd desert in arms be crown'd.)
  The lovely Thais, by his side,
  Sate like a blooming Eastern bride,   10
  In flow'r of youth and beauty's pride.

---

1. **'Twas at**, etc. There is here a sort of rhetorical ellipsis. He means, " It was at the royal feast that what follows happened," or, " The scene of the subject of our Ode was the hall of the royal feast;" but he boldly omits the explanatory clause. In the well-known words, " We met, 'twas in a crowd," the explanatory clause, in fact, precedes; but it is often omitted altogether, as here, especially in the beginning of a tale or poem. Comp. Moore's '*Tis* the last rose of summer."
[When was Persia " won "? See *Hist. Greece.*]
7. At a Greek banquet the guests wer egarlanded with roses and myrtle leaves.
9. **Thais** : See Smith's larger *Biog and Mythol. Dict.* Athenæus is our chief informant about her. According to him, she was, after Alexander's death, married to Ptolemy Lagi. She was as famous for her wit as her beauty. " Her name is best known from the story of her having stimulated the Conqueror (Alexander), during a great festival at Persepolis, to set fire to the palace of the Persian kings; but this anecdote, immortalized as it has been by Dryden's famous Ode, appears to rest on the sole authority of Cleitarchus. one of the least trustworthy of the historians of Alexander, and is, in all probability, a mere fable."
11 [In what two ways may *youth* in this line be parsed? Which is the better?]

Happy, happy, happy pair !
None but the brave,
None but the brave,
None but the brave deserve the fair.   15

II.

Timotheus, plac'd on high
Amid the tuneful quire,
With flying fingers touched the lyre;
The trembling notes ascend the sky,
And heavenly joys inspire.   20
The song began from Jove,
Who left his blissful seats above.
(Such is the power of mighty love.)
A dragon's fiery form bely'd the god;
Sublime on radiant spires he rode,   25
When he to fair Olympia press'd
And while he sought her snowy breast;
Then round her slender waste he curled
And stamp'd an image of himself, a sov'raign of the world.
The list'ning crowd admire the lofty sound.   30
A present deity, they shout around;
A present deity, the vaulted roofs rebound.

---

12. Pair and peer (6) are etymologically identical.
16 Timotheus: See Smith's larger *Biog. and Mythol. Dict.* This Timotheus is said to have been a Theban Suidas tells us he "flourished under Alexander the Great, on whom his music made so powerful an impression that once in the midst of a performance by Timotheus of an Orthian poem to Athena, he started from his seat and seized his arms" The more celebrated Timotheus, "the musician and poet of the later Athenian dithyramb," a native of Miletus, died some thirty years before Alexander's conquest of Persia.
17. Tuneful: See *St Cecilia's Day.* 6
21. Began from Jove: See *St. Cecilia's Day,* 2.
22. Seats: So in Latin. *sedes* is used in the plural
24. [What is meant by *Bely'd the God?* Comp. Shakspere's *Richard III* II ii 76–7.]
For this wild story see Plutarch's *Alex* etc See *Paradise Lost,* ix 494–510 In the mediæval romances about Alexander it was not Jove but one Nectanebus, a refugee king of Egypt, who was the father of the prince: see *e g* the fragment of *Alisaunder* edited by Mr Skeat for the Early English Text Society.
25. Radiant Spires: Comp Milton's "circling spires"
[Which is the better word with which to connect *on radiant spires?*
What does *rode* mean?]
26. Her name was Olympias See *Class Dict.*
31. A present deity. Comp. Hor *Od.* III. v. 2; *Psalm* xlvi. 1.

With ravish'd ears
The monarch hears,
Assumes the god,   85
Affects to nod,
And seems to shake the spheres.

III.

The praise of Bacchus, then the sweet musician sung,
Of Bacchus ever fair, and ever young.
    The jolly god in triumph comes;   40
    Sound the trumpets, beat the drums ;
    Flush'd with a purple grace
    He shews his honest face;
Now give the hautboys breath; he comes, he comes.
    Bacchus, ever fair and young,   45
    Drinking joys did first ordain;
    Bacchus' blessings are a treasure,
    Drinking is the soldier's pleasure;
      Rich the treasure,
      Sweet the pleasure,   50
    Sweet is pleasure after pain.

IV.

Sooth'd with the sound the king grew vain;
    Fought all his battails o'er again;
And thrice he routed all his foes, and thrice he slew the
    slain.
    The master saw the madness rise,   55
    His glowing cheeks, his ardent eyes;

---

37. See Hom. *Iliad*, i. 528-30.
Virg. *Æn*. x. 115:
    " Annuit, et totum nutu tremefecit Olympum."
The Latin *numen* means originally a nod.
36. Bacchus. See *Class. Dict*
43. **Honest face** = handsome face. The epithet is taken from
Virgil.
Honest-like is used in Scotland for "goodly as regarding the person."
44. **Hautboys** = oboes (French, *hautbois*, that is *haut-bois*).
53. [What battles had he fought?]
[What is meant by *to fight over a battle*?]
54. **Ardent eyes:** See Cicero's speech *in Verr*. II iv. 66, of one
Theomastus' madness: "Nam quum spumus ageret in ore, *oculis arderet*,
voce maxima vim me sibi adferre clameret, copulati in jus pervenimus."

And while he heaven and earth defy'd,
Chang'd his hand, and check'd his pride.
  He chose a mournful Muse,
    Soft pity to infuse ;   60
  He sung Darius great and good,
    By too severe a fate
  Fallen, fallen, fallen, fallen,
    Fallen from his high estate,
  And weltring in his blood.   6ɕ
  Deserted at his utmost need
  By those his former bounty fed,
  On the bare earth expos'd he lyes,
  With not a friend to close his eyes.
With downcast looks the joyless victor sate,   70
  Revolveing in his alter'd soul
  The various turns of chance below :
  And, now and then, a sigh he stole,
  And tears began to flow.

            V.

The mighty master smil'd to see   75
  That love was in the next degree ;
  'Twas but a kindred sound to move,
  For pity melts the mind to love.

36. 61. [Was there ever any difference between *sung* and *sang ?* See Latham's *English Grammar*.]
65. **Weltering :** See *Hymn Nat.* 124, (*The Golden Treasury*)
68. **Expos'd**=cast out. Comp Latin *exponere*.
69, Comp. Pope's *Elegy on an Unfortunate Lady :*

    " By foreign hands thy dying eyes were closed:
    By foreign hands thy decent limbs composed."

With not a friend : *A* here has its older force ; it = one, a single ; see note to " at a birth," *l'All. Not a,* is, in fact, a stronger form of *none or no.* The negative in this phrase is sometimes *never*
  73 **A sigh he stole**=he sighed privily, or it may be silently. See Shakespeare's *Taming of the Shrew*, III. ii 142
    " 'Twere good, methinks, to *steal our marriage.*"
  Comp. *Cymb.* I. v 66 :
        " He *furnaces*
      The thick sighs from him ; "
which is explained by " the lover sighing like a furnace " in *As You Like It*, II. vii. 148.
  77. '*Twas,* etc. See above, l. 1.

Softly sweet, in Lydian measures,
Soon he sooth'd his soul to pleasures.   80
War, he sung, is toil and trouble,
Honor but an empty bubble,
    Never ending, still beginning,
Fighting still, and still destroying;
    If the world be worth thy winning,   85
Think, O think it worth enjoying;
    Lovely Thais sits beside thee.
Take the good the gods provide thee,
The many rend the skies with loud applause;
So Love was crown'd, but Musique won the cause. 90
    The prince, unable to conceal his pain,
        Gaz'd on the fair
        Who caus'd his care,
And sigh'd and look'd, sigh'd and look'd,
    Sigh'd and look'd, and sigh'd again;   95
At length, with love and wine, at once oppress'd
The vanquish'd victor sunk upon her breast.

VI.

Now strike the golden lyre again;
A lowder yet, and yet a lowder strain.
Break his bands of sleep asunder,   100
And rouze him, like a rattling peal of thunder.

---

79. [What does *sweet* here qualify ?]
Lydian measures: See Milton's *L'Allegro,* 136.
Conversely, love melts the soul to pity in *Two Gentlemen of Verona,*
IV. iv. 101
82. See Falstaff's catechism, I. *Henry IV.* V. i.
83. [What is it that is *never ending,* etc ? What *fighting still,* etc ?] .
85. **Worth Winning:** So "worth nothing," "worth ambition,"
"worthy sight," "worth inquiry," "worth while" (With "worthy"
the preposition is generally inserted, but in Shakespeare, *Coriol.* III i
299, we have "worthy death ") This construction may be explained in
this way : the Ang.-Sax inflection which marked the word governed by
weorth fell out of use, and its omission was not compensated for by the
introduction of the preposition
96. [What is the force of *at once* here? What does it qualify?]
98. [Why does he say *again?*]
100. **Bands of sleep:** Comp "*bands* of death," "the *bands* of
those sins " (Collect for the 24th Sunday after Trinity), etc. The notes
that rouse him are to be very different from those which are to make
Orpheus " heave his head," in Milton's *L'Allegro.*

Hark, hark ! the horrid sound
Has rais'd up his head;
As awak'd from the dead,
And amaz'd, he stares around.   105
Revenge, revenge ! Timotheus cries,
See the Furies arise !
See the snakes that they rear,
How they hiss in their hair,
And the sparkles that flash from their eyes! 110
Behold a ghastly band,
Each a torch in his hand !
These are Grecian ghosts that in battail were slayn,
And unbury'd remain
Inglorious on the plain;   115
Give the vengeance due
To the valiant crew.
Behold how they toss their torches on high,
How they point to the Persian abodes,
And glitt'ring temples of their hostile gods.   120
The princes applaud with a furious joy;
And the king seyz'd a flambeau with zeal to destroy;
Thais led the way,
To light him to his prey,
And, like another Hellen, fir'd another Troy.   125

VII.

Thus long ago,
'Ere heaving bellows learn'd to blow,

---

108. **See the snakes that they rear**, etc. In _Æn._ vi 571-3,
Tisiphone's left hand is filled with snakes.
117 **Crew :** See _L'Allegro_, 38.
122. **Flambeau :** French words were much affected by the English
in the latter part of the seventeenth century. See Butler :

> "For though to smatter words of Greek
> And Latin be the rhetorique
> Of pedants counted and vainglorious,
> To smatter French is meritorious."

See Macaulay's _History of England._ I chap. iii.
125 [How far does this parallel between Thais and Hellen hold
good?]

While organs yet were mute,
Timotheus, to his breathing flute
            And sounding lyre,   130
Cou'd swell the soul to rage, or kindle soft desire.
    At last divine Cecilia came,
    Inventress of the vocal frame;
The sweet enthusiast, from her sacred store,
    Enlarg'd the former narrow bounds,   135
    And added length to solemn sounds,
With Nature's mother-wit, and arts unknown before.
    Let old Timotheus yield the prize,
        Or both divide the crown:
    He rais'd a mortal to the skies :   140
        She drew an angel down.

---

128. **Organs** : See note on *St. Cæc.* 44.
129. [What is the force of *to* here ?]
133. **The vocal frame** : =the speaking structure.
137. [What is the force of *with* here ?]

MAC FLECKNOE.

Introductory Note.—This piece was directed against Shadwell, the leading Whig poet of the day, as Dryden was the Tory. It was published in October, 1682. Johnson therefore mistakes when he says that it was occasioned by Shadwell's being appointed to succeed Dryden as Poet Laureate (see his *Life of Dryden*) ; for that superseding did not take place till after the Revolution.

In spite of what is said in the following Satire, Shadwell was a comic poet of no mean power, and but for his lavish indecency would well deserve to be read. He was certainly a better play writer than his satirist. Dryden and he had once been friends, and, indeed, fellow-workers, and in those days Dryden had not been blind to his merits In the Epilogue to the *Volunteers*, one of Shadwell's plays, he speaks of him as

" The great support of the comic stage,
Born to expose the follies of the age,
To whip prevailing vices, and unite
Mirth with Instruction, Profit with Delight ;
For large ideas and a flowing pen
First of our times, and second but to Ben."

This praise must have been particularly welcome to Shadwell, not only as coming from whom it did come, but for its form ; for Shadwell modelled himself upon Ben Jonson He, too, aimed at representing " humors." He is said to have resembled him somewhat in person. He found no difficulty in resembling him in his affection for the tavern. Had he lived some half-century sooner he would, no doubt, have gladly been enrolled in what Jonson himself called " the tribe of Ben." If Jonson wrote *Masques*, Shadwell wrote an opera, *Psyche*. In course of time Dryden and he became enemies. Dryden had spoken disparagingly of Ben Jonson (see his *Essay on Dramatic Poetry*) ; Shadwell sneered at *Aurung-zebe.* When the fearful factious excitements connected with the Exclusion Bill and the Popish Plot came to a head in 1678, and the two following years, Dryden and Shadwell were ranged on opposite sides. Shadwell answered the *Medal* with his *Medal of John Bayes ;* he took part also in a lampoon called *The Tory Poets,* aimed at Dryden and Otway. In October, 1682, appeared *Mac Flecknoe · A Satire on the True Blue Protestant Poet, T S ;* and in the following month the Portrait of Shadwell under the name of Og, in the Second Part of *Absalom and Achitophel*

For the name, Shadwell would have been proud to be called the "Son of Ben ; " Dryden calls him the " Son of Flecknoe," the heir of one of the meanest versifiers of the century. Of this poor poetaster, Flecknoe, the very name would now barely be known but for the immortality Dryden thus gave him. Dryden plucked him from oblivion to become a proverb of badness. Thus Swift writes in his *On Poetry, a Rhapsody,* 1744 :

" Remains a difficulty still
To purchase fame by writing ill.
From *Flecknoe* down to Howard's time
How few have reached the low sublime ! "

Besides its great intrinsic merit *Mac Flecknoe* has the additional interest of having mainly suggested the form of Pope's *Dunciad* " I doubt not," says Pope himself in a note to " Flecknoe's Irish Throne " (*Dunciad*, ii 2), " our author took occasion to mention him in respect to the poem of Mr. Dryden, to which this bears some resemblance, though of

14

a character more different from it than that of the *Æniad* from the *Iliad*,
or the *Lutrin* of Boileau from the *Defait de Bouts Rimees* [sic] of Sara-
zin."

ALL human things are subject to decay,
And, when Fate summons, monarchs must obey.
This Flecknoe found, who, like Augustus, young
Was call'd to empire and had govern'd long,
In prose and verse was owned without dispute   5
Through all the realms of Nonsense absolute.
This aged prince, now flourishing in peace,
And blest with issue of a large increase,
Worn out with business, did at length debate
To settle the succession of the state ;   10
And pond'ring which of all his sons was fit
To reign and wage immortal war with wit,
Cry'd, " 'Tis resolved, for Nature pleads that he
Should onely rule who most resembles me.
Shadwell alone my perfect image bears,   15
Mature in dulness from his tender years ;
Shadwell alone of all my sons is he
Who stands confirm'd in full stupidity.
The rest to some faint meaning make pretence,
But Shadwell never deviates into sense.   20

---

3. **Flecknoe :** See *Introduction.*
Augustus was just thirty-three years of age when he overthrew his
formidable rival Antony, and became the undisputed master of the
Roman world   He held that mastership for forty-four years   See *Class.
Dict* or *Hist. Rom.*
8. **Increase :** is often used particularly for family or progeny. See
1 *Sam.* ii. 33   So Shakspere's *Coriolanus*, III iii 114 ; Pope's *Odyssey* ·
              " Him young Thoosa bore, the bright *increase*
              Of Phorcys "
10. **To settle** = the settling   So
              " For not to have been dipt in Lethe's lake
              Could save the son of Thetis from to-die."

(*Two Gentlemen of Verona*, III 1 182) " I leave *to be*," &c. Or *debate to
settle* may = debate how to settle; comp. Milton's *Lye*. 10
    The settling of the succession of the political state was an only too
familiar question at this time   It had troubled Cromwell, it was now
pressing upon Charles the Second, if anything could press upon him,
it was certainly vexing the whole nation. Thus Flecknoe's position was
easy to realize
13 Observe the force of the metre here
    'Tis resolved. Comp. beginning of *Alexander's Feast*
    14 [What " part of speech " is *onely* here ? What does it qualify ?
Where ought it, strictly, to be placed ?]

Some beams of wit on other souls may fall,
Strike through and mako a lucid interval ;
But Shadwell's genuine night admits no ray,
His rising fogs prevail upon the day.
Besides, his goodly fabrick fills the eye   25
And seems designed for thoughtless majesty,
Thoughtless as monarch oakes that shade the plain
And, spread in solemn state, supinely reign.
Heywood and Shirley were but types of thee,
Thou last great prophet of tautology,   30
Even I, a dunce of more renown than they,
Was sent before but to prepare thy way,
And coursly clad in Norwich drugget came

---

22. "The long dissensions of the two houses, which, although they had had *lucid intervals* and happy pauses, yet they did ever hang over the kingdom ready to break forth " (Bacon.)
    Intervall here, as etymologically, of space. Shakspere uses the Latin form in 2 *Henry IV.* V. 1. 85, " a' shall laugh without *interval lums.*"
    24. In a moral sense we still say "prevail upon," =persuade; sc "prevail with." In a material sense perhaps we should rather say " prevail over." Shakspere's *Richard III.*, III, iv. 64. Comp. "prevail against ' Comp also *Daniel* iii. 27 : " These men *upon* whose bodies the fire had no power."
    25. See *Introd.*
    Fabrick : The comparison of a body to a building is common enough; see St. Paul's *Second Epistle to the Corinthians*, v. 1
    26 [Is *majesty* used here in an abstract or a concrete sense ?]
    28. **Supinely :** Keats used *supine* in its original sense in *Eve of St. Agnes.*
    29 **Heywood** was one of the "Elizabethan" dramatists. Of the details of his life little is known. He died some time in the reign of Charles I He would seem to have been a writer of wonderful fertility, for he boasts of having had "an entire hand, or at the least a main finger," in 220 plays. He was a writer of far greater merit than might be supposed from this mention of him by Dryden.
    Shirley : born probably in 1594, died in 1666. Neither to him does Dryden here quite do justice. Lamb says of him, that he claims a place amongst the worthies of this period not so much for any trans-cendant genius in himself as that he was the last of a great race, all of whom spoke nearly the same language, and had a set of moral feelings and notions in common.
    31. **Dunce :** Duns Scotus (he was born about the same time as Dante, died in 1308,) was a man of acute intellect, and of great erudition; but, when that school of learning to which he belonged fell into con tempt, his name became a by-word for ignorance; thus his very emi-nence in his own age placed him in a low and contemptible position in another age. See Trench's *Study of Words.*
    33. **Norwich Drugget :** He wrote first "rusty drugget." (Todd.) Norwich was known for its woollen manufactures in the timo of Henry I., when a colony of Flemings settled in the neighborhood of Worstead "Others, settlers from the same country, joined their breth-ren in the reign of Henry VI. and Elizabeth." (*Pop. Encycl.*) "Wors-

To teach the nations in thy greater name.
My warbling late, the lute I whilom strung   85
When to King John of Portugal I sung,
Was but the prelude to that glorious day,
When thou on silver Thames did'st cut thy way,
With well-tim'd oars before the royal barge,
Swell'd with the pride of thy celestial charge,   40
And, big with hymn, commander of an host;
The like was ne'er in Epsom blankets tost.
Methinks I see the new Arion sail,
The lute still trembling underneath thy nail.
At thy well-sharpened thumb from shore to shore   45
The treble squeaks for fear, the basses roar;
About thy boat the little fishes throng,
As at the morning toast that floats along.
Sometimes, as prince of thy harmonious band,
Thou weildst thy papers in thy threshing hand   50

---

ted," "Lindsey Wolsey," and "Kerseymere" are said to be so called
from East Anglian villages noted for their woollen productions · see
Taylor's *Words and Places* For the term *drugget*, " it is said that drugget or droget was first made at Drogheda in Ireland."
  35. Warbling: See *Hymn Nal* 96.
  Lute: See *Ode for St. Cecilia's Day*, 36.
  Whilom: Scotch "quhylum" This is an old dat. case; so
"seldom." With the help of the prep. was formed from the same stem
the adverb "unwhile," Scotch "unquhile;" see *Piers Ploughman*, Ed.
Skeat, v. 345.
  36. See *Introduction*.
  39. [What other meaning has *well-tim'd*?]
  Barge=pleasure boat. In a "barge" Cleopatra sailed down the
Cydnus; see *Antony and Cleopatra*, II. ii. 196
  42. That is, " such a scene was never depicted even in one of your
own nonsensical plays." Shadwell had written a play called *Epsom
Wells*. The virtue of the springs at Epsom was discovered in 1618.
  45 Well-sharpened thumb: As if thumb was a sword inflict-
ing cruel cuts on the trebles and the basses. Shadwell is the *leader* of
the band.
  [Why do *nail* and *thumb* make the description ludicrous ?]
  49. As they might be supposed to have thronged around Arion ; but in
fact fishes, except seals, are said to be insensible to the charms of music.
  No doubt one great amusement of leisurely voyagers up and down
the Thames in the days of pleasure barges would be throwing over
pieces of bread and toast and watching the eager contentious pursuit of the little fishes. Or, more probably, this passage refers to frag-
ments of the *morning toast* which, thrown out for the benefit of the
swans (a great number of these were kept on the river in the old days),
became objects of desire and pursuit to the fishes
  50. Thy threshing hand: *i. e.* the hand which you move as if
you were threshing = with which you beat time. His roll of "papers"
served him as a *bâton*

St. André's feet ne'er kept more equal time,
Not ev'n the feet of thy own 'Psyche's' rhyme,
Though they in number as in sense excell;
So just, so like tautology, they fell
That, pale with envy, Singleton forswore   55
The lute and sword which he in triumph bore,
And vowed he ne'er would act Vilerius more."
Here stopped the good old syre, and wept for joy,
In silent raptures of the hopefull boy.
All arguments, but most his plays perswade   60
That for anointed dulness he was made.
  Close to the walls which fair Augusta bind,
(The fair Augusta much to fears inclin'd,)
An ancient fabrick rais'd to inform the sight
There stood of yore, and Barbican it hight;   65

---

51. **St. Andre** was a well-known French dancing-master of the day.
52. **Psyche:** See *Introduction*.
54 [What is meant by *they?* and what by saying *they fell like tauto-logy?*]
55. **Singleton** is said to have been leader of the King's private band Pepys mentions how once, in 1660, the king "did put a great affront upon his music, bidding them stop and make the French music play." He was also an actor, as the present passage shows. *Villerius* is a *per-sona* in Sir W. D'Avenant's *Siege of Rhodes* With regard to the *lute and sword*, see the Fifth Act of *The Rehearsal*, where that play is parodied The stage direction runs : "Enter at several doors the Gen-eral and Lieutenant-General arm'd Cap-a-pea, with each of them a lute in his hand and his sword drawn, and hung with a scarlet ribbon at his wrist." Villerius' part required both military valor and musical skill ; hence his double equipment.
62 **Augusta:** As it was the fashion to speak of Charles the Second as Cæsar (see Dryden's lines *To his Sacred Majesty*) and as Augustus (see, e g , his *Threnodia Augustalis*), the capital city of his kingdom came to be called by the affected name of Augusta. It was, in fact, an old name re-vived. Augusta was a common title in the Roman Empire for cities founded or specially patronized by the first of the Emperors ; thus there were Augusta Rauracorum (the modern Aust), Augusta Trevirorum (now Tréves), Augusta Eminta (now Merida), Augusta Prætoria (Aosta), Augusta Taurinorum (Turin), etc. Ammianus Marcellinus informs us that London enjoyed this title. He speaks of " Lundinium, an old town to which posterity gave the title of Augusta."
The walls which, etc.: The old line of the walls may be traced by the gates whose position is still recorded in certain street names, as Lud-*gate*, New-*gate*, Cripple-*gate*, etc Just south of the church of St. Giles', Cripplegate, near the street called *London Wall*, a considerable piece of them yet stands.
63. The strange vicissitudes of the Civil War time, the Plague, the Fire, the suspected instability of the Government, had made London nervous—hysterical, so to speak Hence its wild readiness to believe in Popish plots, etc. See history of Charles II 's reign.
65. **Barbican:** " It was generally a small round tower for the sta-tion of an advance guard placed just before the outward gate of the cas-tle-yard or ballium." "Chaucer useth the word for a watch-tower

A watch-tower once, but now, so fate ordains,
Of all the pile an empty name remains.
Near it a Nursery erects its head,
Where queens are formed and future heros bred,
Where unfledged actors learn to laugh and cry,   70
And little Maximins the gods defy.
Great Fletcher never treads in buskins here.
Nor greater Jonson dares in socks appear;
But gentle Simkin just reception finds
Amidst this monument of vanisht minds;   75
Pure clinches the suburbian muse affords
And Panton waging harmless war with words.
Here Flecknoe, as a place to fame well known,
Ambitiously designed his Shadwell's throne.
For ancient Decker prophesi'd long since   80
That in this pile should reign a mighty prince,
Born for a scourge of wit and flaye of sense,

which, in our Saxon tongue was called a *burgh-kenning* " (Cotgrave.)
For the derivation and first meaning of the word see Wedgwood's *Dict.
Eng. Etym*, according to which barbican and balcony are both but various forms of a combination of two Persian words, meaning an upper
chamber

Hight=was called. Sometimes it has a present sense, sometimes
it is a participle. Spenser uses it frequently in all these ways.
68. **A nursery:** a place where youthful would-be actors, and
perhaps would be play-wrights, made their first attempts, and so the
headquarters of inferior theatrical art
71. **Maximins:** Maximin was the god-defiant hero of Dryden's *Ty-
rannic Love.*
72. Fletcher seems to have been in Charles II.'s reign more popular
than Shakspere In his own day he was placed very near him His
name may be said to stand as for Beaumont and Fletcher. In the plays
written during Beaumont's life it appears almost impossible to separate
his work from that of his colleague, and in those which came after
Beaumont's death (Beaumont died in 1616, Fletcher in 1625), there are
probably posthumous parts.
74. **Gentle Simpkin** was a cobbler in an interlude of the day.
Shoemaking was especially styled "the gentle craft."
75 **Vanished minds**=of intellects departed, of idiotcy. Comp.
Tennyson's.

"O for the touch of a *vanish'd* hand ; "
and " a *vanished* life," in *In Mem.*
76. **Clinches:** In Taylor's *Wit and Mirth* "clinch" is used for a
clencher, "an unanswerable reply" (Halliwell and Wright's Nares'
Gloss.) It was used also for a witty saying, a repartee. (Halliwell's
Dict.) Johnson defines it "a word used in a double meaning, a pun,
an ambiguity."
Suburbian So "robustious" in *Sam. Agon.*, 569; "Mon-
strous," *Faerie Queene*, II xii 85.
77. Panton is said to have been a noted punster of the day
80. **Decker:** Thomas Decker was one of the great Elizabethan

To whom true dulness should some "Psyches" owe,
But worlds of "Misers" from his pen should flow;
"Humorists" and Hypocrites it should produce,   85
Whole Raymond families and tribes of Bruce.
Now empress Fame had publisht the renown
Of Shadwell's coronation through the town.
Rows'd by report of fame, the nations meet
From near Bunhill and distant Watling-street.   90
No Persian carpets spread th' imperial way,
But scattered limbs of mangled poets lay;
Much Heywood, Shirley, Ogleby there lay,
But loads of Shadwell almost choakt the way.
Bilkt stationers for yeomen stood prepar'd   95
And Herringman was captain of the guard.
The hoary prince in majesty appear'd,
High on a throne of his own labours rear'd.

---

dramatists   Jonson is supposed to have satirized him in his *Poetaster*
a compliment which he returned in his *Satiromastix*   Dryden intro
duces him here because he was a "City poet"   Dryden seems scarcely to
have estimated him at his proper worth.   There is a singularly musical
and otherwise exquisite song by him.
    "Art thou poor, but hast thou golden slumbers,"
quoted in the *Golden Treasury*
    83 **Psyche :** *The Miser—The Humorists*, are plays by Shadwell.
    86. **Raymond** is one of the characters in the *Humorists*, "a gentle-
man of wit and honour "
    Bruce is a character in *The Virtuoso*, "a gentleman of wit
and sense "
    90. **Bunhill—** *Watling-street*   See map of London.
    93 **Ogleby :** at first a dancing master, translated the *Iliad*, the
Odyssey and the *Æneid*, besides producing some original poetry, and
writing a *History of China* · See *Dunciad*, i 141 and 328
    95. **Bilkt :** who had been defrauded of their due payments.
    Stationers = booksellers.   This was the original force of the
word, and was still its force in Dryden's time. See Trench's *Sel. Gloss.;*
Dunciad, ii 90.
    Yeomen : " He instituted for the security of his person a band
of fifty archers under a captain to attend him, by the name of yeomen
of his guard "   (Bacon's *Henry VII*)   This word is variously connected
with Fris *gaeman*, a village ; A.-S. *gemane*, common ; A.-S. *yeonge*,
A.-S. *geongra*, a vassal ; fancifully with *yew*.
    � 96. **Herringman** was a well-known publisher of Charles II 's
reign   Dryden in the earlier part of his career, had been connected
with him   He was the " bookseller " meant by Shadwell in his *Medal of
John Bayes* .
        " He turned a journeyman to a bookseller,
        Writ prefaces to books for meat and drink,
        And as he paid he would both write and think."
    98. **Throne :** " state " in the first edition.   " The state was a raised
platform, on which was placed a chair with a canopy over it."

At his right hand our young Ascanius sat,
Rome's other hope and pillar of the state.   100
His brows thick fogs instead of glories grace,
And lambent dulness plaied around his face.
As Hanniball did to the altars come,
Sworn by his syre a mortal foe to Rome:
So Shadwell swore, nor should his vow be vain,   105
That he till death true dulness would maintain,
And, in his father's right and realms defence,
Ne'er to have peace with wit or truce with sense.
The king himself the sacred unction made,
As king by office and as priest by trade.   110
In his sinister hand, instead of ball,
He plac'd a mighty mug of potent ale;
" Love's Kingdom " to his right he did convey,
At once his sceptre and his rule of sway;
Whose righteous lore the prince had practis'd young   115
And from whose loyns recorded " Pscyhe " sprung.
His temples, last, with poppies were o'erspread,
That nodding seemed to consecrate his head.
Just at that point of time, if fame not lye,
On his left hand twelve reverend owls did fly.   120
So Romulus, 'tis sung, by Tyber's brook,
Presage of sway from twice six vultures took.

---

99. **Ascanius:** See *Æneid*, passim. Dryden did not produce his translation of Virgil's great poem till some fifteen years after the coming out of *Mac Flecknoe*, but he was already thoroughly familiar with it, as, indeed, all his age was.
100. **Rome's other hope** = spes altera Romæ (*Æn*. xii. 168).
101. **Glories:** See Keats' *Eve of St. Agnes*.
103. See *Class. Dict.* and *Hist Rome*.
104. [What does *sworn* mean here ?]
107. [What is meant by his *father's right* ?]
108. [What is the government of *to have*, etc.?]
109. **Made** = performed
111. **Ball :** " Hear the tragedy of a young man that by right ought to hold the *ball* of a kingdom ; but by fortune has made himself a ball, tossed from misery to misery, from place to place "
113. **Love's Kingdom :** a play by Flecknoe. Derrick says he wrote four plays, but " could get only one of them acted, and that was damned "
    Convey is used here in its technical sense "The Earl of Desmond, before his breaking forth into rebellion *conveyed* secretly all his lands to feoffees in trust."
116. **Recorded** = above mentioned ; or rather = sung, for *Psyche* was an opera " *Record*," to sing ; applied particularly to the singing of birds. A recorder was a flageolet.

The admiring throng loud acclamations make,
And omens of his future empire take.
The syre then shook the honours of his head,   125
And from his brows damps of oblivion shed
Full on the filial dulness ; long he stood,
Repelling from his breast the raging God ;
At length burst out in this prophetic mood :
"Heavens bless my son ! from Ireland let him reign 130
To far Barbadoes on the western main ;
Of his dominion may no end be known
And greater than his father's be his throne ;
Beyond ' Love's Kingdom ' let him stretch his pen !"
He paus'd, and all the people cried " Amen."   135
Then thus continued he : "My son, advance
Still in new impudence, new ignorance.
Success let others teach, learn thou from me
Pangs without birth and fruitless industry.
Let ' Virtuoso's ' in five years be writ,   140
Yet not one thought accuse thy toil of wit.
Let gentle George in triumph tread the stage,
Make Dorimant betray, and Loveit rage :
Let Cully, Cockwood, Fopling, charm the pit,
And in their folly show the writers' wit.   145
Yet still thy fools shall stand in thy defence,
And justify their author's want of sense.
Let 'em be all by thy own model made
Of dulness, and desire no foreign aid,
That they to future ages may be known,   150
Not copies, drawn, but issue of thy own.

---

126. [What is meant by *damp of oblivion* ?]
127. [What is the force of *full* here ?]
128. **The filial dulness**: Comp Horace's "mitis sapientia Læli,"
etc.
135. [What are the ludicrous points of this line ?]
136. Comp. *Æn* vi 95.
138. *Ile* is parodying *Æn* xii 435.
140 " While Dryden accuses Shadwell of slowness in composition.
Rochester attributes his faults to haste "
142 **George** = Sir George Etheredge, a man of fashion, a diploma-
tist, a poet, a comedy writer. He died at Ratisbon, where he was Minis-
ter Resident, in 1694.
143. **Dorimant, Loveit**, etc , are characters in Etheredge's plays,
The Man of the Mode, and *Love in a Tub*.

Nay let thy men of wit too be the same,
All full of thee and differing but in name.
But let no alien Sedley interpose
To lard with wit thy hungry Epsom prose.   155
And when false flowers of rhetoric thou wouldst cull,
Trust nature, do not labour to be dull ;
But write thy best and top ; and in each line
Sir Formal's oratory will be thine.
Sir Formal, though unfought, attends thy quill   160
And does thy northern dedications fill.
Nor let false friends seduce thy name to fame
By arrogating Jonson's hostile name ;
Let father Flecknoe fire thy mind with praise
And uncle Ogleby thy envy raise.   165
Thou art my blood, where Jonson has no part ·
What share have we in nature or in art ?
Where did his wit on learning fix a brand
And rail at arts he did not understand ?
When made he love in Prince Nicander's vein   170
Or swept the dust in Psyche's humble strain ?
Where did his muse from Fletcher scenes purloin,
As thou whole Etheridge dost transfuse to thine ?
But so transfused as oil on waters flow,
His always floats above, thine sinks below.   175
This is thy province, this thy wondrous way,
New humours to invent for each new play :
This is that boasted byas of thy mind,
By which one way to dulness 'tis inclined,

---

154 **Sedley** : Sir Charles Sedley was one of the wits, the poets and
the dramatists that sparkled in the court of Charles II
155. **Hungry** = lean, " scrannel." See Milton's *Lycidas*, 125.
Epsom prose refers to Shadwell's *Epsom Wells*.
159. Sir Formal Trifle is a verbose, oratorical person in Shadwell's
Virtuoso
161. " By the *northern dedications* are meant Shadwell's frequent dedications to the Duke of Newcastle ; he dedicated also to the Duchess,
and to their son, the Earl of Ogle "
163. See *Introduct*
170. **Nicander** is a character in *Psyche*.
174. Observe the rhyme between *purloin and thine* So join was
sounded *jine*, etc. *Noise* rhymes with *cries* in *Dunciad*, ll 221-2.
178. **Byas** : See Shakspere, *Richard II*. III. 'v. 5 ; *Hamlet*, II. l.
66.

24 MAC FLECKNOE.

Which makes thy writings lean on one side still,   186
And, in all changes that way bends thy will.
Nor let thy mountain belly make pretence
Of likeness ; thine's a tympany of sense.
A tun of man in thy large bulk is writ,
But sure thou'rt but a kilderkin of wit.   185
Like mine, thy gentle numbers feebly creep ;
Thy tragic Muse gives smiles, thy comic sleep.
With whate'er gall thou sett'st thyself to write,
Thy inoffensive satyrs never bite ;
In thy felonious heart though venom lies,   190
It does not touch thy Irish pen, and dyes.
Thy genius calls thee not to purchase fame
In keen Iambicks, but mild Anagram.
Leave writing plays, and choose for thy command
Some peacefull province in Acrostick land.   195
There thou may'st wings display and altars raise,
And torture one poor word ten thousand ways ;
Or, if thou would'st thy diff'rent talents suit,
Set thy own songs, and sing them to thy lute."
He said, but his last words were scarcely heard,   200

---

182. **Tympany :** i. e., no healthy normal growth, but a dropsical expansion. The meaning is exactly illustrated by what Macaulay says of Dryden's own plays in his Essay on Dryden " The swelling diction of Æschylus and Isaiah resembles that of Almanzor and Maximin no more than the tumidity of a muscle resembles the tumidity of a boil The former is symptomatic of health and strength, the latter of debility and disease."

191 [What does *dyes* mean here ?]

193. **Keen Iambicks :** that is, satirical poetry such as Archilochus wrote " proprio iambo." " Hence also the Iambic verse is now so called, because in this metre they used to *Iambize* [i. e. satirize] each other."

Mild Anagram : See *Spect.* Nos. 58 and 60, where these lines are quoted, and chronograms and "*bouts rimez*" are also discussed : but anagrams and acrostics were much older than Addison supposed. See also Disraeli's *Curiosities of Literature*, on "Literary Follies ; "— "I shall not dwell on the wits who composed verses in the form of hearts, wings, altars, and true-love knots : or, as Ben Jonson describes their grotesque shapes,

'A pair of scissors and a comb in verse.'

Tom Nash, who loved to push the ludicrous to its extreme, in his amusing invective against the classical Gabriel Harvey, tells us that ' he had writ verses in all kinds : in form of a pair of gloves, a pair of spectacles, and a pair of pot-hooks,' " etc.

For Bruce and Longville had a trap prepared,
And down they sent the yet declaiming bard.
Sinking he left his drugget robe behind,
Borne upwards by a subterranean wind.
The mantel fell to the young prophet's part, 205
With double portion of his father's art.

---

22. 201. Bruce and Longville, in the *Virtuoso*, make Sir Formal Trifle
disappear through a trap-door in the midst of his speechifying

2

A SONG FOR ST. CECILIA'S DAY.

Introductory Note. This song was written for the festival of St. Cecilia, 1687. The celebration of that festival by lovers of music was commenced (or revived, if, as is probable, it was kept in some sort before the Reformation) in 1683, in which year Purcell " set " the song that was written for the occasion In 1684 Oldham wrote the anniversary song, in 1685, Nahum Tate ; in the following year the festival was not observed ; in 1687 Dryden wrote the song given in the text. He wrote another, his *Alexander's Feast*, ten years afterward Pope wrote in 1708.

It is not clear how St. Cecilia came to be regarded as the patron saint of music. In her legend, as told in the *Legenda Aurea* (written toward the close of the thirteenth century), almost literally translated by Chaucer in his *Secounde Nonnes Tale*, she is not so spoken of. All that is said there of music is that " Cantanibus organis illa in corde suo soli Domino cantabat," etc., or in Chaucer's words, 12,062-5, ed. Wright ;

> " And whil the organs made melodie,
> To God aloon in herto thus sang sche :
> ' O Lord, my soul, and eck my body gye
> Unwemmed, lest that I confounded be.' "

Of course, however, the Latin words might be translated, ' while her organs were sounding ; " that is, " while she was playing." The legend goes on to say, that this " mayden bright Cecilie " was under the immediate and present protection of an angel. In this passage of her story may, perhaps, be seen the beginning of the tradition referred to in *Alexander's Feast*, and so exquisitely painted by Raphael and others, that " she drew an angel down ;" but in the old story, not her sweet playing, but her spotless purity, brought the angel near her, not to listen, but to be a " heavenly guard." He is seen by her husband, too, when he becomes a Christian ;

> " Valirian goth home and fint Cecilie
> Withinne his chambre with an aungel stoude
> This aungel had of roses and of lille
> Corounes tuo, the which he bar in honde ;
> And first to Cecilie as I understonde,
> He gaf that oon, and after can he take
> That other to Valirian bir make."

She and he are said to have suffered martyrdom in the year 220 All, then, that the legend certainly shows to the purpose is, that St. Cecilia was one over whom music had great influence—that it inspired in her high religious emotion It may show, further, that she was herself a skilful musician. The fame of her deep passion for sacred music, and possibly of her skill in it, might well, at a later time, give countenance, if it did not give rise, to the tradition that she invented the grand instrument of church music

As for this said instrument, its early history is obscure. " Some derive its origin from the bagpipe ; others, with more probability, from an instrument of the Greeks, though a very imperfect one—the water organ—as it is known that the first organs used in Italy came thither from the Greek empire It is said that Pope Vitellanus (died 671) caused organs to be set up in some Roman churches in the seventh century. Organs were at first portable. The organs now in use are consid-

ered an invention of the Germans, but respecting the time of this invention, opinions differ. . . . It is certain that the use of organs was not
common before the fourteenth century " (*Pop Cycl*) That the name is
Greek is a strong confirmation of its Greek origin. "The only incident
of religious history," runs a paragraph in Chambers' *Book of Days* (i
495), "connected with the 10th of April that is noticed in a French work
resembling the present, is the introduction by King Pepin, of France,
of an organ into the Church of St. Corneille, at Compiègne, in the year
787."

I.

FROM harmony, from heav'nly harmony
This universal frame began.
When Nature underneath a heap
Of jarring atoms lay,
And cou'd not heave her head,   5
The tuneful voice was heard from high:
Arise, ye more than dead.
Then cold and hot and moist and dry
In order to their stations leap,
And Musick's pow'r obey.   10
From harmony, from heav'nly harmony
This universal frame began ;
From harmony to harmony
Through all the compass of the notes it ran,
The diapason closing full in Man.   15

---

1 This was an opinion said to have been held by Pythagoras : "We
find running through the entire Pythagorean system the idea that order
or harmony of relation is the regulating principle of the whole universe "
(Smith's larger *Biog Myth Dict*) It was not only "the regulating,"
but in the first instance the creative principle ; it brought into union
opposing elements, "jarring atoms " The music of the spheres was a
Pythagorean notion. See Milton's *Hymn Nat*. 125
[What does *heavenly* mean here ?]
   2. **Frame:** This was a favorite word with poets about the close of
the seventeenth century See "vocal *frame*," in *Alexander's Feast* :
"a shining *frame*" in Addison's
       "The spacious firmament on high," etc.
Began from, etc : See *Alexander's Feast*, 25 :
       "The song began from Jove "

5. **Heave her head:** See Milton's *L'Allegro*, 145. Miltonic words
and phrases are very common in Dryden's writings. Pope, too, has this
phrase, *Dunciad*, ii. 256 .
       " Rous'd by the light, old Dulness *heav'd the head*."

6. [What is the force of *The* here ?]
   Voice = words uttered by the voice.
8. See *Paradise Lost*, ii 898
14. **The notes:** i. e. of the first seven notes of the octave.
15. **The diapason:** " Diapason denotes a chord which includes all"

II.

What passion cannot Musick raise and quell?
When Jubal struck the corded shell,
His list'ning brethren stood around,
And, wond'ring, on their faces fell
To worship that celestial sound;   20
Less than a god they thought there cou'd not dwell
Within the hollow of that shell,
That spoke so sweetly, and so well.
What passion cannot Music raise and quell?

III.

The trumpet's loud clangor   25
Excites us to arms
With shrill notes of anger
And mortal alarms.

---

tones; it is the same with what we call an eighth or an octave; because
there are but seven tones or notes, and then the eighth is the same again
with the first." See Milton's *At a Solemn Music*, where he would that
we on earth should "answer" the melodies of heaven,

> "As once we did, till disproportion'd sin
> Jarr'd against Nature's chime, and with harsh din
> Broke the fair music that all creatures made   ,
> To their great lord, whose love their motion swayed
> In perfect *diapason*," etc

Closing: See *Hymn Nat* 100. So Herbert:

> "Sweet spring, full of sweet days and roses;
> A box where sweets compacted lie,
> My music shows you have your *closes*,
> And all must die."

16 Collins, in the beginning of his *Ode* describes how, when Music
was yet young,

> "The Passions oft, to hear her shell,
> Throng'd around her magic cell,
> Exulting, trembling, raging, fainting," etc.

till at last each one determined to try his own skill. Comp. *Midsummer
Night's Dream*, II. i. 150, the well-known line,

> "Music hath charms to soothe a savage breast."

Quell is strictly but the older form of *kill*.
17. **Jubal**: See *Genesis*, iv. 21
Shell: This somewhat affected name for a lyre found great favor
with our poets from Dryden till the close of the last century. It is of
course a Classicism
The chorded shell: See Homer's (so assigned) *Hymn to
Mercury*, 25-65.
28. [What does *mortal* mean here?] See Trench's *Select Glossary*, s.v.
Comp.:

> "Come, thou *mortal* wretch."

[*Antony and Cleopatra*, V. i. 63.]

The double double double beat
Of the thundering drum　　　　　　　　　　30
Cries, heark : the foes come !
Charge, charge, 'tis too late to retreat !

IV.

The soft complaining flute
In dying notes discovers
The woes of hopeless lovers,　　　　　　　35
Whose dirge is whisper'd by the warbling lute.

V.

Sharp violins proclaim
Their jealous pangs and desperation,
Fury, frantick indignation,
Depth of pains and height of passion,　　　　40
For the fair, disdainful dame.

VI.

But oh ! what art can teach,
What human voice can reach
The sacred organ's praise ?

---

33. Chaucer says of his Squire :
　　" Syngynge he was or flowtynge all the day."
The " floyte " is mentioned in the *House of Fame*
　34　[What does *dying* mean ?]　Comp　*Twelfth Night*, I 1 4.
Discovers= simply uncovers　See *Merchant of Venice*, II. vii 1:
　　" Go draw aside the curtain, and *discover*
　　The several caskets to this noble prince."
Comp　*dis*robe, *dis*people, *dis*mantle, etc.　[In what sense do we use the
word *discover* ?]
　35　[How does the sense of *hopeless* here differ from that in Shakspere's
Richard II I. iii 152, " the *hopeless* word of ' never to return ' " ?
　36. " The lute was once the most popular instrument in Europe, al-
though now rarely to be seen except represented in old pictures. . . . It
has been superseded by the guitar," etc.
Pope follows Dryden in his
　　" In a sadly pleasing strain
　　Let the warbling lute complain."
　37. **Violins** : Violin (= violino) is a dim of viol, as violoncello of
violin　The violin completely replaced the viol in the reign of Charles
II.　See Chappell's *Pop. Mus.* ii. 467-9
　41. **Dame** : Comp　Milton's *Paradise Lost*, ix. 612 :
　　" Sovran of creatures, universal *dame.*"
So often in Shakspere.
　44. **Organs** : See Milton's *Paradise Lost*, i. 708, vii. 596 ; Shakspere's

Notes inspiring holy love,   45
Notes that wing their heav'nly ways
To mend the choires above.

VII.

Orpheus cou'd lead the savage race,
And trees unrooted left their place,
Sequacious of the lyre ;   50
But bright Cecilia rais'd the wonder high'r :
When to her organ vocal breath was giv'n ;
An angel heard, and straight appear'd,
Mistaking earth for heav'n.

GRAND CHORUS.

As from the pow'r of sacred lays   55
The spheres began to move,
And sung the great Creator's praise
To all the bless'd above :
So, when the last and dreadful hour
This crumbling pageant shall devour,   60
The trumpet shall be heard on high,
The dead shall live, the living die,
And Musick shall untune the sky.

Tempest, III. 98, "the thunder—that deep and dreadful *organ-pipe* "
The older English poets generally speak of organs, or a pair (= set) of
organs: that is, the word orga= denotes but a single pipe. Thus San-
dye :
"Praise with timbrels, *organs*, flutes ;
Praise with violins and lutes."

33. 47. The audacity of this line may be regarded as a sign of the
times, which were not reverent nor humble-minded. See Dryden's *Ode
to the Memory of Mrs. Anne Killegrew*.
48 **Orpheus**: See Shakspere's *Two Gentlemen of Verona*, III. ii.
78–81 ; *Henry VIII*. III. i. 8 , etc.
50. **Sequacious**: Comp Sid. *Carm*. xvi. 3: " Quæ [cheylys] saxa.
sequacia flectens." Comp. Ovid's " saxa *sequentia*," *Met*. xi. 2.
52. [What is meant by *vocal breath* ?]
53. Comp. *Alex. Feast*, 170
Straight: See *L'Allegro*, 69.
55. See note on l. 1.
60. Comp. Shakspere's *Tempest*, IV. i. 15-16.
63. U**ntune** = destroy the harmony, i. e. the vivifying principle.

Lightning Source UK Ltd.
Milton Keynes UK
UKHW021214301219
356115UK00008B/2269/P